Healing
with Spirit

Healing
with Spirit

Saleire

Winchester, UK
Washington, USA

First published by Sixth Books, 2012
Sixth Books is an imprint of John Hunt Publishing Ltd., Laurel House, Station Approach,
Alresford, Hants, SO24 9JH, UK
office1@jhpbooks.net
www.johnhuntpublishing.com
www.6th-books.com

For distributor details and how to order please visit the 'Ordering' section on our website.

Text copyright: Saleire 2011

ISBN: 978 1 78099 557 1

A CIP catalogue record for this book is available from the British Library.

Design: Stuart Davies

Printed and bound by CPI Group (UK) Ltd, Croydon, CR0 4YY

.

We operate a distinctive and ethical publishing philosophy in all
areas of our business, from our global network of authors to
production and worldwide distribution.

CONTENTS

About the Author vi

Introduction 1

Chapter 1: Why do we need healing? 3

Chapter 2: Types of Healing 7

Chapter 3: The Spiritual Healer and Spirit 20

Chapter 4: Spiritual Healing and the 'Code of Conduct' 24

Chapter 5: Becoming a Channel 27

Chapter 6: The Ideal Healing Room 33

Chapter 7: My Experiences 35

Chapter 8: Heal without Healing 47

About the Author

Saleire is a healer, artist, medium and published author. She was aware of Spirit since childhood and realized that she was also healing as a child, coming from a dysfunctional home life, she quickly learned how to sense the atmosphere and to pray for healing for her family.

She studied the bible and devoured every book on spiritual awareness she could find to enhance her knowledge of the other side and the healing entities, such as Angels and Guides. She wanted to know more about this *something* that left her and knew this was the way forward.

Saleire's journey has taught her that to heal others you must heal yourself first. Aware that something was guiding her, she was not surprised to learn that it was Spirit, encouraging us toward self-healing, becoming whole again and to share that healing energy with others.

She hopes this book will help you find your healing and wishes you love and light on your journey.

I am healed by the love of my beautiful family:
Arie, John, Joe and my darling grandsons.
I love you.

I am healed by the love of my beautiful family:
Arie, John, Joe and my darling grandsons.
I love you.

Introduction

I am delighted to share with you some of the knowledge I have gained over the years of healing. Spiritual healing is a gentle process; none of this shake, rattle and roll, ridding you of demons here. The spiritual healer knows that he is just the channel and allows the healing to flow to you without any kind of commotion. Healing is a gentle communication between your spirit and those on the other side that administer the healing energy and the healer is just the phone-line so to speak.

Spirit is just waiting to help you heal yourself and those around you. They want you to be happy and rid yourself of the inner pain and trauma of your lives. If you can be open to this healing, you will walk with your head held high and feel a strength you never knew you had. We all need healing, but it takes personal responsibility to actually go and seek it. This book helps you onto that path of self-healing.

I want to dispel any fears you may have of entering a spiritualist church or organization to receive this kind of healing. Some people think there are spirits there about to jump on them as they enter, but this is not so, they wait until you are in the healing room to do that. No, I am kidding. If you go to a church to receive healing, you do not need to be a member or even attend the services there. You can walk in off the street, have healing, and leave again with no fuss whatsoever.

This book covers the basics of other therapies and an easy guide to working with the chakras. I will show you how to use color and crystals, among other things, to energize these centers. We are living spirit and within us are the communication centers of the body, mind, and spirit. Without proper care and energy renewal, these centers can become depleted causing dis-ease in the body.

I will share my experiences of healing and how the spirit works with you, not only to heal the complaint but the source of the complaint, the inner healing that we all need. I give you examples of this.

There is a healer in all of us. We have the knowledge and compassion to become healers of our family, and ourselves. This book shows you how to use this healing ability and what to expect when you are the channel. It will also give you guidance on setting up a healing room that will enhance any patient's experience.

I hope, just by reading the book, it will be a healing experience.

Chapter 1

Why do we need healing?

Within the body is the Spirit, a spiritual double so to speak and within this body of light there are portals, called chakras that are constantly swirling around assimilating the life-force energy. They receive energy, transmit energy, are the communication centre of the spirit, and control our spiritual, mental, and physical welfare. The chakras are the portals in your aura, the electromagnetic energy field that surrounds every living thing. We usually replenish this energy field through the food we eat and through the rays of cosmic energy from our environment. Sometimes though, this is not enough and our energy becomes depleted to the point of us needing healing.

Spiritual healing is a universal energy sent from the source, through the healer to the patient through these chakras.

Imagine you are an electrical appliance with several ports from which to acquire electricity, the USB plug, the actual plug from the wall or the batteries. These ports are like the chakras in your energy field and we depend on these ports to draw in the energy we need to survive. If a port is damaged, the appliance will not work and the same applies to chakras. Too much emotional anxiety, drugs, or severe pain can damage the chakras, they can begin to leak the life-giving energy, and this in turn can shut down the body in disease. This is when healing is most definitely needed. The healing energy can be taken in through any chakra, but your own spirit will decide which chakra to attend to first.

Once the healing energy is given, the patient's own spirit

takes over and applies the healing to wherever it has the greatest potential to heal. For instance, you might have a headache, and of course, the pain is in your head, but that is not where the body needs healing. You lost your job; you are worried and afraid of what the future might hold. You try not to think about it, but the brain knows that you have to cope with it somehow, so it produces a physical pain, hence the headache. Your spirit knows this and sends healing, *not* to your head, but to the chakra that controls emotions, as this is where it really hurts.

The healers are mere channels for those on the other side who administer this wonderful energy. In fact, most healers like the word channel, as this is more appropriate. They know the actual energy comes directly from Spirit, through their spiritual centre, out through their hands and minds to the patient.

Think of Spirit as the source of energy, the socket so to speak, the healer is the wire that leads to the patient and the patient is the actual appliance.

Here is a basic idea of the chakras, where they are, what they govern and what can go wrong if they are imbalanced:

Crown chakra: Top of skull – Spiritual connection
Governs: Brain, muscular and central nervous system.
Blocked: Depression, brain tumors, headaches, confusion, and disassociation with the body.
Healthy: Feeling spiritually connected to all living things. Intelligence, open-mindedness, an ability to retain knowledge and a greater sense of awareness.

Third Eye: Brow - Intuition
Governs: Eyes, ears, nose, face, sinuses, pineal and pituitary gland.
Blocked: Nightmares, eye, ear and nose infections, inability to

remember dreams, poor vision and poor imagination
Healthy: Intuitive, perceptive, remember dreams, psychic abilities, strong imagination

Throat Chakra: Neck - Communication
Governs: Throat, neck, mouth, teeth, vocal chords and the jaw
Blocked: Not being able to express your feelings, weakness in vocal chords, hoarse, throat infections, pain in jaw, neck problems, gum infections and thyroid problems
Healthy: Ability to express yourself, communicates well, good voice and strong neck muscles

Heart Chakra: Chest – Emotion
Governs: Heart, lungs, immune system, upper back and bronchial tubes
Blocked: Withdrawn, depression, sadness, fear of intimacy, and shyness
Healthy: Compassionate, loving, caring, balanced and at ease in relationships

Solar Plexus: Below the diaphragm – Will Power
Governs: Digestive system, liver, gallbladder, stomach, pancreas and adrenal system
Blocked: Poor digestion, fearful, low self-esteem, weak willed, sluggish and low on energy
Healthy: Confident, respectful, ability to meet challenges and inner harmony felt within

Sacral Chakra: Lower abdomen – Sexuality
Governs: Intestines, pelvis, kidneys, sexual organs, lower back and prostrate
Blocked: lack of passion, desire, frigidity and fear of change
Healthy: Ability to experience excitement and pleasure, self-nurturing, healthy sexual appetite

Root: Base of spine – Survival

Governs: Immune system, base of spine, legs, bones, and feet.

Blocked: Bowel disorders, leg pain, lower back pain, skin problems, lack of energy, inability to relax and fear for security

Healthy: Grounded, sensible, ability to find harmony, vitality, and trusting of others

If you want to know if your chakras are blocked just hold the palm of your hand an inch or so away from them, if they are working correctly you will feel a slight tingle in the centre of your palm, if they are blocked you will feel nothing. If this is so, try moving your hand in a circular motion around the centre of the chakra. Sometimes this helps to get the energy moving again. This might take a bit of practice and you will need to become sensitive to the energies emanating from the chakras, but in time, you will master it and know exactly which chakras need healing.

Why do we need healing? We are energy, we are light, and through the difficulties of life, we can lose that energy, or find it depletes easily in a world of stress. When we are in love we are full of energy, could climb a mountain and still have energy to go dancing, that's because when you are in love the energy flows from you to the one you love and back again. You become more psychic, as in; you just know he is going to call. You smell a rose as if it is the first time you did, and life seems so much more exciting. You are glad to be alive.

We should be feeling on top of world, raised to your highest height, full of joy and loving every minute of it, yet all too often, this is not true because of our lack of energy and a stressful world. That is why we need healing.

Chapter 2

Types of Healing

In this chapter, I will give you a brief idea of what kind of healing you might expect from each individual healer, or therapist. They are all wonderful, but in the end, they all do the same thing, which is give energy to the chakras and get the energy flowing again.

Magnetic Healing

This is merely the transference of healing energy, from one person to another. The only trouble with this kind of healing is that it can leave you feeling exhausted. It is always better to ask Spirit to do the healing and you become the channel. When you love someone, you automatically send out this kind of nurturing to each other, this is why people keep searching for their soul mate to make them feel complete. Complete, as in fully energized, full of life, full of the light giving energy and love, complete in mind, body, and spirit.

Many parents give magnetic healing to their children when they are sick. They have such sympathy and love for the child that they send out healing energy without even knowing it. They would rather take the pain on themselves than watch their child suffer.

Whilst lending a shoulder to cry on you also send out some of your vital energy to another through sheer empathy. It is not life threatening. It will only leave you feeling a little tired, but if the person needs a lot of healing, you might feel quite drained. This is why it is always good to ask the source to work through you. I am sure we have all had a friend or neighbor that has left us feeling a bit drained.

Absent Healing

This kind of healing reaches the patient through the power of thought and prayer together. The healer asks the source to send healing energy through them to the patient. Distance does not matter, even if the patient remains unaware that healing is on its way, the cosmos is like a huge network of energy lines to which we are all connected. It is *the intent* that is the most important thing here. Visualization helps the healer to imagine the patient in a well state rather than sickly. This is more positive and helps you to focus on them feeling better than being sick. Positive thought is necessary to help the healing process.

If the patient knows of the healing on its way to them they can help by opening up to the energies by relaxing, breathing in the energy and knowing that it surrounds them in light.

Thought is real and it does reach the person at the other end of our thoughts. We send well wishes to newlyweds, birthday wishes and condolences, all with the intent of making the other person feel better, enjoy life, or just be happy. This is thought, and therefore, in a sense, absent healing. When we see an accident we usually say, "Oh my God! I hope they are okay!" in addition to these words, we send out sympathy, love, and healing to the people in the accident. Whether we know it or not, we are constantly sending out some form of healing energy to each other through empathy. Because we are connected through our spiritual selves, we love each other and therefore there are no strangers in the spiritual world. If you want to send out healing on larger scale, make it known to those in the Spirit world that you want to be a channel for that moment in time and let it flow.

Color Therapy

Color also emanates energy. In spiritualist centers, where

Spiritual phenomenon happens a lot, the curtains, cushions and even the carpet becomes faded as Spirit use the energy in the color of the fabric to help build the energy in the room. Therefore, you can use color to energize the chakras too. Try wearing a blue jumper or t-shirt if you are feeling unwell. Blue is a very healing color. It will calm you. Try red if you need energy and pink if you are feeling a little unloved. People power dress, usually in black, to show an air of authority. Doctors dress in white coats, which give them an air of cleanliness and sterility. We have all put on that little red dress to feel sexy.

You can use colored water crystals to bathe in, wrap a lovely colorful scarf around your neck if you want a boost or even concentrate on a color and visualize it entering the chakra relating to that color. Keep the colors light and bright and use something you can really imagine, like a big red tomato or fresh, green apple. Keep it simple; just let it flow in through the front of your chakra and out through the back, passing through the centre of the chakra, giving it all the energy it needs.

This is how energy works; white light holds the complete spectrum of colors within it. Energy is light and this is what we need to stay balanced. We must have sensed this years ago before we knew anything really about chakras and energy. We say things like; I feel blue, seeing red, tickled pink, she looks a bit green around the gills, or green with envy. We often associate a color with a feeling, a sickness, or the mentality of the person at the time. Red has always been associated with 'a fallen woman' or angry person because it is associated with the root chakra, the base chakra, our basic, passionate self. They probably did not know this at the time the association began, but these sayings do not come from nowhere.

Light boxes are used in color therapy. We need light in our lives; we are often depressed in the winter and need the light of spring to cheer us up. In fact there is a name for it, S.A.D very appropriately, Seasonal Affective Disorder, where the lack of light really does affect our mood in the winter even though our mental health is perfectly okay throughout the rest of the year. Light boxes are a good way to get light into your world. You can buy or rent a Light Box, which sends out light as close to daylight as possible with colored filters to heal whichever chakra that color resonates with the most.

You can do this color therapy exercise at home. Take a glass of water, preferably in a colored glass, or buy a color filter from a color therapist and leave it on the window for a couple of hours in the sunshine. Then, let the sun do its thing. The energy from the rays of light helps the water absorb color from the glass or filter, infusing the water with that energy. When you sip this water it should help, or you could even bathe in it. This is called solarised water.

Alternatively, if you do not want to go to the trouble of finding a colored glass or filter, then take a piece of cloth that matches the color of the chakras and place that color over the chakra. This works well too.

When you are choosing the wallpaper, or paint, for your walls at home, think about color therapy and think about what you need to help you achieve the calmest atmosphere in your home. The same goes for duvet covers. We spend at least seven hours a day in bed, so choose a color that you feel you will achieve the most relaxed sleep in. White is always a good color as it holds within it the full spectrum, but can be too austere, just as blue can be too cold. Try to pick a warm, cozy color to help you sleep well, but not red, as this can make you feel agitated.

Crystal Healing

Healing with crystals is a very good way to heal the chakras. Each crystal emanates the energy needed for each chakra to energize itself. The crystals correspond to the color associated with the chakra. Just lay the crystals on, or near the chakras and relax as they absorb the energy.

Crystals are powerful stones and if you use them correctly can provide some wonderful energy around your home to keep it calm and full of light. Enjoy them, take care of them and they will return the favor. If you just want a general one to begin with, buy the clear quartz as this has within it the full spectrum of colors and is very good for clearing the energy field of any emotional debris.

Here are some more facts about crystals that you might not know and will help in the healing process. Crystals are living energy, some talk about the spirit of the crystal and I cannot see why that should not be as it is full of the life force that is spirit.

One of the first indications that we have been using crystals for ceremony and protection is in the bible. Aaron's breastplate is famous for its 12 crystals placed upon a breastplate, with the name of each of the tribes engraved up on it, for him to wear in the temple – Exodus 28 15-21. There is also a mention of crystals when the lamb on the throne is seen for the first time, in Revelations chap. 4-5 'He who was sitting was like a jasper stone and as sardius in appearance, there was a rainbow around the throne like an emerald in appearance...' Both Sardius and Jasper are red stones and of course, used as a symbol here to show God's wrath at sin and as God is the universal energy, which is white light, then there would be a rainbow of colors as white is the full spectrum of color. Therefore, you see, we have been fascinated with crystals for a very long time.

I will not go into every crystal here, as it would take too long, but here are a few to get started with.

Crown chakra   White/Gold   Diamond/Clear quartz

Third Eye chakra	Indigo	Azurite/Amethyst
Throat chakra	Blue	Lapis lazuli/Sapphire
Heart chakra	Green/Pink	Rose quartz/Emerald
Solar Plexus	Yellow	Amber/Tiger's Eye
Sacral chakra	Orange	Fire opal/Amber
Root chakra	Red	Ruby/Garnet

Crystals are used for protection, to bring love, and so much more. Investigate and find the one that is right for you. When you are buying a crystal, hold it in your palm and see if it vibrates. If it is full of energy, you might feel a tingle in your hand. If it doesn't it might not be the right one for you or it needs energizing. You can do this by leaving in the sunlight for a few hours, some are sensitive to the light, so use the moon to energize these or put it under a running tap or even wash them in the sea, as this is a great way to energize them. There are more ways to cleanse, program, energize and even store your crystals, so please do investigate.

Reflexology and Massage

Reflexology is a special kind of massage for your feet. On each foot, there are zones that correspond to every organ in the body and if massaged can release the blocked energy in that area and so, aid healing. The same goes for regular massage, if the energy is moved it will shift any blockages in the energy field, aiding circulation and so the flow of energy around the body. Makes sense, so get massaging, and enjoy the feeling of all the wonderful, life-giving energy filling your body. Everyone knows about massage in one way or another, so I will not go into detail here; after all, this book is a basic guide to get you on the road to healing yourself and those around you.

Meditation

This is a tool for healing that is centuries old. Every one of us at some time or another has used it. When you are washing the dishes and go into that trance-like state, you are in a sense, meditating. Your mind is blank and for a few seconds you are not there. Time goes by unnoticed and you are in the zone. The same applies when you are reading a book, the house could fall down around your ears and you wouldn't even notice. This is the purpose of meditation, to block out the world, make your mind a blank canvas, and leave all that stress behind.

I find the best way to meditate is to go to a park, let the energy of the trees balance your chakras while you meditate on the scenery. You will find that the stresses of the day just leave you because you will not be able to focus on them as you did before. It's as if everything slows down and the brain takes a well-earned rest.

There are so many ways to meditate, but in general, all you are trying to do is relax your brain. But that little voice keep taunting you with, 'You forgot to do the washing up', 'Shouldn't you be paying attention?', 'You need to get the shopping in' and so on. It will try to distract you from relaxing because it does not like to lose control. Therefore, to relax, tell your brain to take a hike, you are having some down time, and eventually, if you ignore it, those voices will fade into the background and you will feel the peace wash over you.

Meditation is all about breathing. Breathe deeply and release, do it a few times and see the difference in how you feel. Be careful though, if you are a shallow breather, as I am, you might get a rush of blood to the heart that can make you feel a bit dizzy. Take it nice and slow. Breathing deeply is very good for releasing blocked energy as it gets the circulation going.

Tree Hugging

I know it sounds funny, but tree hugging does work. The energy flowing through a tree from the earth is amazing. I once had a very bad backache and didn't have any painkillers with me. I spotted a huge oak tree and leaned against it, while asking it to heal me. It did, and not only that, it gave me some extra energy to get on with the day, as I had been very tired.

Nature is full of ways to heal. Try lying down on the grass, letting all that lovely green energy balance your emotions and ask Mother Earth to let her energy flow through you. She is just one big ball of nurturing energy, so hold on to your hat when she gives you healing.

Herbal Remedies

Herbs have been used for remedies since the year dot and there are several for each ailment. We have all used them at one time or another. Aloe Vera, found in after-sun creams to help soothe sunburn. Arnica, used to prevent bruises and we have all had a cup of camomile tea to calm our nerves. There are a whole host of herbs to use if this is your way to heal or if you want to heal yourself, but do be careful how you prepare them and note if they have any side effects. Investigate thoroughly and do ask a herbalist which ones are best for you.

To cleanse the energies the North American Indians use a technique, called smudging. They made a smudge stick, which is a stick with white sage bound onto it and then burned it. The smoke is then wafted around the room for purification. Incense works in the same way.

Aromatherapy

Speaking of herbs, Aroma therapists use these in their essential oils. The aroma of such oils are said to have a beneficial effect on the body bringing a sense of harmony and peace. I have a tendency to believe in this because of this one reason, when you go into a house that has just baked bread you get a warm, fuzzy feeling in your chest. This is a well-known fact and that is why they have tried to produce these same aromas in air fresheners. If a person wants to sell their house, it would be a good idea to bake some bread before the potential buyers come, because it does have a tendency to make you feel at home and if this works, they might buy your home.

Smell a rose on a summer's day and tell me that you don't go, 'AH', and take in a deep breath, which in turn releases stress. So, next time you are out try buying a wonderful scented candle or some delicious freshly baked bread.

An oil burner is a little gadget that you can also use to fill your house with a gorgeous aroma. As the candle heats the oil, it releases a heavenly perfume. It can be quite strong, so try to find one that you can live with. Lemon is deliciously fresh, but I find that musk is a bit too pungent for my taste. Try to think of a fruit or flower that you really like the scent of and find an oil with that scent.

Yoga

Yoga controls the body and mind to bring them into harmony with the Spirit. Through breathing exercises and body positions, you can find a peace of the soul that no other exercise can bring. It truly is a wonderful practice to release blocked pathways of energy, improve the mind and the physical body, but also to increase your awareness of your spiritual being.

There are so many types of Yoga used today but the one I will talk about is Kundalini Yoga, which is a focusing of breath and posture to bring about Kundalini Awakening, in basic terms, to make the chakras open fully and allow the energy to flow through them.

Kundalini is said to be like a snake coiled around the base

of your spine. A powerhouse of energy within and once released, it rises to the top of the head, close to your spine, opening the chakras one by one. As each chakra opens, you experience different levels of awakening, along with a mystical experience, until it finally reaches the crown chakra where the mystical experience is said to be sheer bliss.

Self-awakening I would call it, god consciousness, or just becoming aware that you *are* spirit is enough to awaken the Kundalini. Focus on bringing your spirit into play into every part of your life and awareness will follow. The power within you is the god-given energy that we can all call upon to rise up and let us experience the reality of our existence. We are that power, we just don't know it yet, and when that power rises and unites with the universal power, it *will* be bliss because you will realize that you are one with the universe and all within it.

To bring about Kundalini awakening, focus on the chakras one by one. Start with the first one, the base chakra, and work your way up. You will feel the energy rising or as I saw it like a tube with little lights within it rising up and down at the same time, bringing energy from the earth to the crown chakras and back to the earth again. It is truly something that we should all be doing because we need to feel connected to the source as often as we can.

I would say that this is the basic idea of Yoga but please do try this one as not only is it good for your soul, it is essential for keeping the muscles nice and supple and your body feeling the way it should.

Spiritual Healing

Spiritual healers are certainly not ministers who cast out demons and slap you on the forehead! They would never call you a sinner, because they know that the healing process is through positive thought, learning to love yourself and most certainly not through thinking of yourself as a sinner and begging for mercy. A true healer would never bring something so negative into play.

Spiritual healing is achieved when the channel asks his guides or spiritual beings on the other side to administer healing through him and then gets out of the way. He is a passive channel and does not bring the ego into play during the process of healing. He is just on stand-by while the real healers do their thing. As I said before, the energy is channeled through him, to his hands and on to the patient. He must not let his thoughts or, need to know the outcome, block the energy. He just allows the energy to flow through him. A good healer can do this with ease, as a good healer does not bring ego into the healing room.

The healing forces applied to the patient's inner spiritual centre works outwards, through the seven subtle bodies of light to the physical. The seven bodies are:

Etheric Body

This body is closest to the physical body. This expands about two inches from the body. It is misty gray in color and is a duplicate for your physical, meaning it has all the organs within it.

Emotional Body

This one is associated with our feelings. The colors within this body are multi-colored and change according to our mood. It expands approximately three inches from our body.

Mental Body

Our thoughts and mental processes are within this body. It expands at least eight inches from the body and the color is usually a bright yellow.

Astral Body

This very subtle, light body reaches out about nine to ten inches from the physical body. It is a rainbow of colors and stars. I once saw this body as I was practicing astral travelling. It was a body made of stars, billions of tiny stars of brilliant white. It was incredibly beautiful.

This body is the one you travel with, from one dimension to another.

Etheric Body

This body is one of the three lighter bodies; the energy vibrates at a higher frequency than the lower bodies. This one extends at least 15 inches into in the auric field. It is blue in color.

Celestial Body

When you meditate and feel divine love for all living things, you have reached the sixth body, associated with the heart chakra. We can experience bliss through this amazing body of light.

Causal Body

Shaped like an egg this beautiful body expands outward to around three feet. It is golden and once again, I have seen this body of light. It truly is something to see, the gold sparkles like sunshine on rippling lake and is full of light and beautiful energy. It vibrates very quickly. When you have reached the seventh body you know you are one with God because of the love you feel, it truly is unconditional.

I have seen these bodies whilst healing, but one of the most spectacular things that ever happened to me was when I meditating on the aura and suddenly I felt like I was spinning, but was perfectly still. Something like a rod of light shot through my body and made it rigid and then it began spinning at an incredible speed until I no longer felt the spinning. At this point, I knew I was in the centre while the spinning was all around me. I felt so calm, and at one with the universe and God.

The healing energy passes through these bodies straight to the centre and then expands outwards to the physical. That is why the effect is not often immediate, it sometimes makes a few stops along the way, but it will always get there in end.

I would recommend this kind of healing to anyone. The energy is complete, from Spirit, through Spirit, to Spirit. There is no need to energize it, like crystals, it is just there whenever you need it. It has such a lovely warm feeling to it and relaxes not only muscles but the brain as well. Suddenly all the worries in the world just fade away and you feel stronger and more able to cope. I have seen wonderful things whilst being a Spiritual healer, which I will tell you about later on in the book.

To receive Spiritual healing you would have to go to a Spiritualist church. The healers are trained to a high standard and work by the 'Code of Conduct' set out by the Spiritualist National Union. The healers there work for nothing, but you can give a donation if you like.

You will find a list of Spiritualist churches on the internet, there are many all over the world. Just look up when the healing days are. You do not have to make an appointment to have healing or become a member; you just walk in and ask for healing. You may feel the energy, or you may not, but I know this, you will begin to feel better, even if it is not immediate.

Chapter 3

The Spiritual Healer and Spirit

We all have the potential to be a healer. A person who has reverence for all living things has an even greater potential. Humanitarians who wish to alleviate other people's suffering know that time on earth is only fleeting and to make it a meaningful life, they must share love, joy, hope and peace with their fellow human beings.

A good channel for healing will try to keep their energy balanced and full of love, as they know it can change the conditions around them and this, in turn, helps others. Acutely aware of how their words and actions affect others they keep them positive and loving. The psychic link will be strong because of a compassion and deep concern for the welfare of humanity.

Through mediation and attunement, they have learned to trust their instincts and have found an inner peace, which is quite evident in their persona. Their inner light shines out to all and infuses love and compassion into every situation.

On tuning in to the Higher Intelligence, the healer learns that becoming a channel requires self-seeking, self-discipline and complete honesty to cleanse any negative energy built up from past regret, guilt or suffering and truly begins to love and heal the child within to become a clearer channel for the healing energies.

Once the channel eliminates ego and learns to be still they replace this ego with trust in Divine Spirit and eliminates themselves from the process of healing allowing the energies to flow completely uninterrupted.

The peace and devotion to service that surrounds a good

healer can be felt. They are often confident and calm in their dealings with patients because they know that Spirit will guide them in word, thought and action during the process of healing.

Kind, patient, gentle in their approach, understanding and considerate in every thing they say and do, devoted to Spirit and knowledgeable in his job as a healer, for me, gives the healer a gold star.

A good healer never, and I mean never, tells you that you are cured, because that is not their job to do so. The Spirit heals, not the healer and only the Spirit knows the outcome of that healing session, unless they have given the channel some insight, but in general, it's not down to the channel to say you are cured.

For example, if a patients emotional stability is fragile, let us say, through suffering a loss as a child or not being nurtured properly, symptoms may develop because deep inside them is a need to be healed emotionally, even if they do not know it stems from their loss in childhood.

Let's say, chronic chest pain is their complaint with no real physical evidence. They have seen a doctor, had the tests, but nothing shows up, and so they come to a healer to help them.

Spirit knows that this pain is merely a manifestation from the patient's inability to cope with their lack of nurturing in childhood and therefore the chest pain is not an immediate concern.

The patient does not understand that the pain is a cry for help and the caring and understanding they so desperately need. They are unaware it is caused from trauma in childhood; however, their Spirit does know and wants the real cause of the pain to be healed and not the manifestation. Therefore, the chest pain will not be dealt with until his emotional needs are addressed and strength is given to deal with the underlying issue. Spirit knows that the chest pain will go as soon as the patient becomes aware of the trauma and seeks help to resolve this issue and not the chest pain, only then can the real healing begin. A good healer must be aware of this and tell the patient that healing always works, but how and when is up to your spirit.

A healer knows that both your spirit, and the spiritual beings who administer the healing energies, work together for the good of your *whole* being. These spiritual healers do not want you to suffer and will help you face any traumas in your life. They want you to rid yourself of guilt and regret and the fear of not being loved or some other fear that you hold deep within your being.

Negative emotions prevent you from having a happy life. Through self-seeking, you can see what really ails you; is it a backache or is someone being a real burden around you, a neck ache or someone in your life being a 'pain in the neck', is it chronic chest pain or a lack of love in your life. Rid yourself of any negative emotion that has built up in your aura and you rid yourself of the pain. This is the only way to be truly healed and if you ask your spirit to show you where you need healing it will.

A proficient healer is a good listener and will try to comfort you, but is not a counselor; on the other hand, sometimes a good chat is all that is needed to make you feel better. Some people think they have to be mentally ill to go to a counselor, but that is nonsense. Sometimes people just need to see their problem from another perspective and a counselor is qualified to help patients sort out problems that they cannot cope with on their own. Your doctor can assign a counselor if you need one, so don't be afraid, what do you have to lose, but the pain of emotional trauma.

I should point out here that if you do suffer from chest pain you should always go to your doctor to get it checked out. Chest pain might be due to depression, or even anemia, but it is always wise to get it checked by a professional to rule out anything serious.

I would recommend that you go to all three for the best possible chances of healing. The Doctor, counselor and healer can get to all the areas that need attention and after all, it's your life that we are talking about here and why shouldn't you be the happiest you can be.

We all have the potential to be a healer, but your first responsibility is to yourself and your own healing. Your life is about self-discovery, finding out who you are and what makes you tick. It is about shedding any negativity from your life and learning as much about the real you, the happy you, the loving you, as you possibly can.

As a child, we laughed until we fell over, danced for joy, and sang aloud all the way home from school. A child does not worry about the embarrassment of falling over, or what people think of them, they just live for the moment and experience life with great enthusiasm. We are still that child, but now we are suffocating in a web of social expectation. We are told to conform to what other people need to feel comfortable around us, we are asked to behave according to their rules, but to heal yourself you have to clear that web and free yourself to be truly happy. You are the healer of your own lives, so be the best healer you can be and work hard to be kind to yourself as you go along the path of seeking *you*.

Chapter 4

Spiritual Healing and the 'Code of Conduct'

To become a Spiritual healer you only need two things, compassion for human suffering and a desire to help. The rest is a matter of choice, whether you want to heal with an organization like the Spiritualist National Union, The National Federation of Healers or the Corinthians is up to you. Whichever one you choose, you will have to follow 'The Code of Conduct'. This is an important document and all healers have to follow it to the letter. It states clearly, if you practice spiritual healing the you must abide by the rules of the 'code of conduct' and those rules define a spiritual healer as a channel for the forces and energies from the world of Spirit, only to be administered through the laying on of hands, through prayer or thought from a distance. At no point in this healing, should there be any other form of contact with the body through massage, manipulation, or physiotherapy. No diagnosis, herbs, prescription, or promise of a cure and absolutely no derogatory remarks regarding the patient's treatment from the medical profession or current medicine. Otherwise, it states, you are in much danger of breaking the law.

In 1970, the Guild of Spiritualist Healers had their first meeting and in 1973, a set of byelaws was drawn up. Spiritualist healers now had a committee to guide them. When the SNU was established in 1994, they issued a membership card and a copy of 'The Code of Conduct' to their healers. The spiritualist healer who followed this code was now protected against accident and public liability providing they followed it to the letter.

'The Code of Conduct' gave spiritualist healers a new kind of professionalism in the knowledge that they were behaving in the correct way, both morally and legally. It protected the patient from fraudulent charlatans who would proclaim a gift for cures at a very high price, to the detriment of the patient's health, and brought respect from the medical profession.

Sadly, I have seen healers who did not follow this code of conduct and was horrified. There will always be the healer who thinks he is beyond the law, just as there are doctors who break the law, but it is up to you to take the right action in such cases. Report them or they will carry on doing a terrible injustice. The 'Code of Conduct' is a good start to eliminating this kind of behavior and any organization that does not provide you with one should not be considered if you decide to train as a healer.

If you choose to go it, alone you will have to consider insurance for the security of yourself and the patient, as is the case for all therapists. The patient's welfare must always be your first concern but you could become liable if they have an accident in your healing room or some such mishap, so insurance is essential.

However, if you choose to be a healer with an organization you will need training in a variety of things with an examination at the end of it. Try not to let this put you off, as they are as simple as doing your homework. Read the materials sent to you, study them and *know* them. A good healer should know the legal/safety requirements, how to treat patients with the utmost respect whilst in his care and his behavior must comply with the 'Code of Conduct' set out by the organization.

How you tune in to Spirit as a channel is up to you, but in general, the actual healing is a laying on of hands and this should be done with the utmost respect for the patient. In fact, there is no real need for a healer to touch the patient as healing can be transferred to the patient from a couple of inches or so from the body.

Chapter 5

Becoming a Channel

Becoming a channel for healing is one of the most rewarding things you will ever do. How you tune in to Spirit is up to you, as is the laying on of hands, or not, whichever way you choose, it should be done with the utmost respect and consideration for the patient. Healing can be transferred to the patient from a couple of inches so it really makes no difference to the healing process.

So, let me show you what a general healing session would entail, it is a quick guide to how you should begin to heal. This is just a basic guide, how you heal and how the healing comes through will be up to you and your guides. However, this will set you off on the right foot.

First, you should always begin by washing your hands. This breaks the link with the last patient and prepares you for the next. It is also more hygienic.

One of the most important things for a healer to ask the patient is if they have consulted a doctor regarding their complaint. If not, you should always recommend that they do. Healing and medicine work alongside each other. The healing administers work with doctors also; some illnesses need a quick cure with medicine, which is what the patient might need at the time. However, in the end, it is up to the patient to decide what they want to do. Once that is done, you are ready to begin the healing session.

You start by making the patient comfortable. Ask them to remove their glasses as a precaution; you do not want to knock them off during healing. Explain to them the procedure, how you will start, whether you will touch them or not (ask permission to do so) and how you will finish the healing session. It helps them to know this so they can fully relax. If they are very tense, chat a little, make them feel at ease, have them breathe deeply a couple of times and allay any fears they might have.

Once you have done this, you put your hands on their shoulders and ask permission from their spirit to go ahead with the healing. This opens the channel and lets the patient know you have begun. You could also work from the Crown chakra first but try not to touch the head as sometimes your hands can be quite heavy, let the patient feel the energy instead of your hands. Once this chakra is open you can begin to work on the rest of their body in succession by placing the palm close to the chakra at the front and the other palm at the back of the body, this helps to unblock any chakras and allows the energy to flow through them.

You will feel the chakra open and will feel the energy flow. If the chakra is open, the energy just flows through the chakra with ease. You will feel as if something is leaving your hand, a pulling sensation toward the chakra. If this chakra is blocked you might feel as if you have been pushed away or no energy at all. To open this chakra, try moving your hand in a circular motion to get it going, and wait and see, it might take time to feel anything, but you will. Do not be surprised if you are not sensitive to the energies yet, it might take a bit of practice.

You might get a sense or vision of something wrong with the chakra, like a big knot tied in it, or it looks like a ball of string. You might see color or sense a feeling with a chakra. These are just ways to show you what is going on. A ball of twine knotted up can show how the emotions are, or a stomach might be knots because of something they are keeping locked away, either way, spirit show you these things to help the patient later, but do not beat yourself up if you don't understand them yet. That will come in time too.

If, when you are finished healing, the patient asks you what you found, and you say, you're stomach is in knots through nerves, this might just explain what they were feeling and put aside any fear they might have had. You will find the right way and the simplest way to work with your guides and which symbols help you understand what is going on as quickly as efficiently as possible.

Don't be surprised if you get an image of something a bit odd. I once had an image of the man actually beating himself over the head with a book. Now I could think either he was completely insane but usually there is a sense of what the image means. I sensed he was writing a book, possibly on something to do with the head, like psychology or the like and that he was unsure if the knowledge he had was enough. I told him exactly what I had seen and what I thought it meant. He was delighted. It turns out that he was a psychologist and had written a book about psychology and was worried what his peers would think of it. Thankfully, I had also seen him surrounded by doctors clapping their hands. Therefore, he got the answer and the healing he needed to go ahead with his book.

This healing was not only in the energies flowing from spirit to his spirit, but also in the chat at the end of healing. You should always ask the patients permission to give any messages or images you receive while giving healing. Some people can't feel a thing during healing but when they are told something that you have seen and could not possibly have known about; it becomes the icing on the cake, and to be honest, is all that is needed in some cases. They not only know that they are on the way to healing, but that spirit know of their concern and are trying to help them with it. It becomes more personal then.

As you work down the chakras you should also work on the body to keep the energy flowing. Place a hand on the shoulder and the other on the elbow; allow the energy to flow from your one hand to the other. This brings the energy down through the arm and unblocks as it goes. Now place one hand on the elbow and one on the hand. This allows the blocked energy to flow through the fingers and out of the body. You could also just put your hands on theirs and do it this way, asking the energy to flow. Either way, you will feel the energy flowing through the tips of the fingers.

When you reach the elbow joints or other joints, you might feel red-hot heat in your hands. This is often the case when the patient has arthritis. They will feel this sometimes and find it hard to describe. It does not burn or feel uncomfortable; it is more concentrated and goes right to the source of pain. If the patient has bruising or a swollen joint from a sports injury it can often feel like ice within your hand, or a piercing cold energy, but again, not unbearable for the patient or healer.

Now move on to through chakras and see what you can sense of feel as you go along. If you want to imagine a color or a light going into the chakra that is up to you and all visualization is a good too to aid healing, but I like to sense what the chakra is telling me instead of what I am sending to the chakra. The chakra is a communication centre and it will tell you what it needs in the best possible way for you to understand, so try to listen.

When you have reached the base chakra, do not touch the person, it is not appropriate and can make the patient feel very uncomfortable. No healer should touch these sensitive areas. In this case, channel the energy from a few inches from the body. This works just as well.

The hips are the next place to unblock energy that might have built up. Once again, place a hand on the hip and the other on the knee and let the energy flow through, and then from the knee to the feet, allowing the blocked energy to leave the body.

Blocked energy in the body, when cleared, is sometimes felt like tiny little electrical shocks to the body. I once gave healing to my sister and her chakras were blocked. She kept flinching throughout the healing and afterwards said she felt little shocks running through her body. So don't be worried if this happens, it is just the energy releasing and it a good thing.

Sometimes you will feel the pain in your hand, and might even take on some of the pain yourself during a session or perhaps the mindset of the patient. This is to help you understand what the patient is going through. Imagine if you could go to the doctor and instead of trying to explain a pain, you could somehow show him through it manifesting in his body for a few minutes. This can happen whilst giving healing. Do not worry that you will take on this pain permanently, as soon as you wash your hands at the end of the session, you will release this energy.

Healing is complete, now go back to the crown chakra, and ask for it to be closed and surrounded with light. Thank Spirit for the healing and for using you as a channel. Now gently, rest your hands on the shoulders of the person and close down the session. This also prepares the patient to come to their senses as they might feel a little dizzy or drowsy from the healing energies.

Give the patient time to recover fully before you talk to them, be gentle, and allow them time to make sense of it all. When they do open their eyes, you can chat about your findings and once again, allay any fears they might have about what they experienced during the healing.

Now wash your hands and let the energies of that person leave you. If you don't do this you can become confused when you bring a sense of the last patient with you to the next patient, so please do cleanse the energy and begin afresh. You should also cleanse the healing room after each session. Ask

Spirit to clear any residual energy left over from the healing sessions so that your room is now spiritually energized and ready for the next day of healing.

There are many variations of how to heal, what you might experience and how your guides will work with you, but this is a basic guide as to what you might expect. Like I said, don't worry if you do not feel anything for the first few times you heal, this is normal, but give it time and your guides will work with you towards a great healing relationship.

Chapter 6

The Ideal Healing Room

If you want to be a healing practitioner of any kind, you must have an inviting healing room. The room itself can make a difference to how the patient feels. First impressions can either make the patient nervous or feel at home. If you go to someone's house and their couch is full of cat hairs, their cups are dirty and the person smells of onions and garlic, would you feel comfortable sitting down to tea. No, of course not, and the same goes for a patient who comes to your home for healing.

A healing sanctuary should be just that, a place of refuge where people come to escape the strain of everyday life, a peaceful, friendly environment where they can regain their inner peace. They should be greeted with warmth, understanding, and compassion. As beautiful as it can be to lift their hearts and strengthen their spirits.

Décor should be in warm pastel shades with soft lighting and a comfortable chair to sit in when they first come inside. Gentle music can also create a peaceful atmosphere in a room. The room must be spotless and the healing couch covered in with clean, fresh linen. White linen is fine, but can be a bit too sterile, so maybe try a light fresh color, like lemon or peach. Towels are necessary also; they are needed for many things, like when the patient comes in out of the rain.

Artificial flowers are best, but must be dust-free. Allergy sufferers will thank you for this. Hot water is a must in any healing room to cleanse your hands after each patient's healing session is over. Tissues, placed in several places so the patient does not have to hunt for them and some cleansing wipes in case they have a good cry and their mascara runs. The wipes should be of the non-allergic type and fragrance free. If you have any pretty ornaments that you want in your healing room, please make sure you dust them regularly. Freshness is the key to a lovely healing room.

If you have a waiting room, you could place information of the treatments you give and your card, but no tatty magazines or dust-ridden books.

In all cases, the carpets or rugs should be secure as this could be a safety risk. You will have to consider these things when you are dealing with the public. A fire extinguisher should be close to hand. Install a new one, as a dusty old one does not give the impression of professionalism. The patient should feel safe, so no creaky floorboards that wobble or carpets with holes in them, this can be a danger to elderly patients. You might want to think about wheelchair access and install a ramp if necessary. If there is a heater or fire in the room, keep it guarded. Pay attention to whether the room is too hot or too cold, either one can be annoying whilst receiving healing.

And last, but not least, always have a shower, check your breath and your clothes for odors, because believe me, there is nothing worse than a healer who is close to you, breathing all over you and smells of the dinner they just ate. Clothes should be fresh and again, not smelling of the dinner you just cooked. Try to see it from the patient's view and provide them with the best possible healing experience you can.

As a Spiritual healer you would have to follow, a 'Code of Conduct', and I would hope that this applies to all therapists, but if not, try to consider what it embarrassing for the patient and treat these issues with sensitivity.

A happy patient is well on the way to becoming a healed one.

Chapter 7

My Experiences

I trained as a Spiritual healer many years ago, but I would not say that I became a healer then; I just learned the rules and regulations that came with the training course. I became a healer from the time I was aware of other people's suffering. The first time I hugged my mother when she was crying and wished I could take away her pain was the day I became a healer. You can feel it, it's as if something leaves your body, and goes to the person who is suffering. Of course I know now that is was energy, but as a child I just knew that something left me and went to my mum and it felt good, but exhausting. Now I know that this was magnetic healing. I did this so many times that in the end I just knew before she was going to be sad and I would pray that someone would come and help her, and in that sense, became the channel for that healing to come through.

I was a sensitive child, to every little creature and to those around me. Every living thing, including my teddy bear, had feelings as far I could see and it was my mission that these feelings would not be hurt by me if I could help it. I had seen so many people in my life being hurt that I did not want to inflict this pain upon anyone. If I could, I would try to take away my siblings pain by memorizing their favorite songs, or remember things that were important to them to let them know that I cared. I think back now and I know I was healing from the time I can remember.

I was an odd child and in that I mean, I loved playing at being a priest, nun, nurse or a teacher, which were not the usual games children played. They were my favorite games of all time. I would tie a lace curtain around my head and hey presto, I was a nun. My mother had a wonderful velour table-cloth, which acted well as the altar cloth, and I used her cup that she won for running as the chalice. I would read the whole mass and do all the actions much to my family's surprise. They did not understand my need to care for others and my need for spiritual enlightenment. Even as a child I would ask my mum questions about the bible, which I read profusely, but all I got back was, don't ask so many questions.

My family could not understand why I hated the violence and anger about me and I could not understand their need to hurt each other. I wanted to be different. I had seen too much pain for one young life. I wanted to make a difference in the world, even if that was only to be gentle with every living thing and be kind to them. I thought if I did this they would be happy, but sadly, the world does not work like that.

As a child, my guides were close, even though I did not know it at the time. I would practice yoga positions when I was too small to know even the word, Yoga. I would dance like a Native American Indian when I had lit the fire, with such grace and intricate steps, that my sister was flabber-gasted when she saw me doing it for the first time. I knew there were people in the room when the light was switched off and was always scared of the dark because I did not under-stand who these people were.

However, they were always watching over me as this story shows. When I was about two years old, my mother left a friend to watch over me, as she thought I was dying. I could not breathe and had a rash all over my body. I had pneumonia. My mother had seen this before, so she rushed to get the doctor.

When she got back, I was sitting up in bed with not a care in the world and the rash was gone. My mother's friend was sitting there speechless and her face was as white a ghost. She told mum that she was praying for me and suddenly passed out, and when she woke up, I was sitting up with not a worry in the world.

Many years later, a medium told me that my life had been saved as a child. That I was very sick and Spirit had come to heal me through another person in the room. They said they healed me but left me too sensitive, as the environment I grew up was too rough. They apologized. I laughed when I heard that. Oh! Boy, were they right, but the interesting part about this story is my mother's friend passing out. She was praying, which is really asking to be a channel for healing, and they probably sent her to sleep so they would not give her too much of a shock and to get on with the work without any interruptions. Either way I am glad they did.

When I grew up I had many hard times, some, no human being should suffer, but in the end, it made me a better healer. I had felt the pain of abuse and utter despair and therefore could understand the pain my patients suffered. I learned that loving others is not enough, you have to learn to love yourself first, that is the most important thing, because if you don't love yourself, no matter how nice you are, others will not respect you and you will suffer because of this. The best thing I learned through those bleak years was that love endures, not the love of others, but the love within you and if you can keep that alive, you have not lost a thing. If you can remain as loving as you were as a child, you will have lived a life that makes you feel proud.

At 18, I entered a Poor Clare monastery in the continued search for spiritual enlightenment, but soon left as I found that most nuns are just women in a habit, just as some priests are just men in a habit. Saying that, there are real nuns, the ones with a vocation and a heart so full of love that they almost shine with golden light. I met two such nuns whilst in the monastery. They both kept in touch with me after I left and until they passed to spirit, but they were an inspiration to me and I loved them dearly, not because they were nuns, but because they were decent, kind, and gentle human beings.

Years later, I was told that the only reason I went to the monastery was to meet one of my guides, who happened to be my Mother Superior and the wonderful thing was that the medium gave me her full name too. I was delighted to hear that, as Mother Ella was so full of light and a healing presence when she walked into a room. There are no coincidences.

So, you see, if you are a healer, the spirit will guide you along the way. They won't make your life easier for you, but they will try to guide you in the right direction to finding peace within and that is more important than any riches.

I really started to see and hear Spirit when I was 20. I felt a girl sit on the end of my bed and I shot up like a rocket when I heard her say that it was all going to be okay. I was terrified. The people in the dark when I was a child hadn't spoken to me, so this was a first. As time went on, I saw a fully manifested spirit and I began to realize that they were coming through for something other than to scare me half to death. I began to search my soul for the answer. The one thing I noticed was how many people had told me that I was a healer, or had a healing influence on them. My mother used to comment on the warmth of my hands, saying they were so hot and when if I gave a massage to my family they would say that the pain had left them.

I knew something left me when I wanted to make people feel better, so I set out to learn what that something was and read as much as I could about the healing energies and the spiritual realm. I also tried very hard to reach my guides.

The first guide to come through was my Native American Indian guide, Sparrow Hawk. He came so close that I became him, meaning through clairsentience as if he manifested over my body. He showed me a past life where I had been with him where, through no fault of his own, he could not protect me and I was killed. Therefore, he came to tell me that he *would* protect me in this life and that was the beginning of a long and wonderful relationship with Sparrow. He is my rock when it is hard to be spiritual and my guardian when something does not feel right in the energy. He is the one that most people see when I am channeling healing. He protects my family and my home and is truly a very strong spirit.

I have many guides and helpers that come through whilst I am giving healing and tuning in, but the one that really is a genius is my doc. Dr Hans Shultz is German and was a surgeon when he was alive. When I am giving healing, sometimes, my doc pops in to let the patient know he is doing the healing.

One time, I was giving healing to a patient and she said she could not feel anything and asked me what she should feel, I was about to tell her that she could try relaxing a bit more and not concentrate on feeling anything when she nearly jumped from the chair. I knew what was wrong, as I had seen the Doc touch her knees. She jumped up and looked around but there was only her and myself in the healing room.

I said, my doctor touched you on your knees, and she looked like she was going to faint. 'How did you know that?' she shrieked. I explained that she had been complaining that she wasn't feeling anything, so my Doc obliged and touched her knees.

This girl had been a heroin addict and within one month of healing, she was no longer an addict. She took her life in her hands and took control of it again. That is the wonder of healing. In fact, the last time she came to me for healing, I saw Doc take off his white coat and put it around her shoulders. I knew she had felt it because she looked at her right shoulder as he did it. When the healing was over she told me that she had felt something being put on her shoulders, I told her that it was his white coat and again, she was speechless because she said whilst I was giving her healing she was thinking of becoming a healer herself, hence the Doc giving her a white coat. I love it when Spirit does something like that, it shows they are completely with you and often have such a great sense of humor. They would not do this if they knew she would have been scared to death.

There will be guides who swirl around the room, like my Spanish dancer who is dressed in a fabulous, ruby-red dress and dances around the room to build up the energy, or my nun who comes when the patient needs a very gentle approach. There are many guides who will work with you and help you with healing the patient, some you will know, some you won't, but if you trust in them, they will be there to teach you.

That was my path to becoming a healer. It is a frustrating path at times, especially when you are learning to step out of the way to let them heal through you. Humans are nosey and want to know what is going on, but to be a healer you have to trust in the Spirit.

In my case, they told me at the beginning of the healing session or sometimes before it. I am clairaudient, so I can hear Spirit, so as soon as I put my hands on their shoulders I would listen and they always told me the problem, often times it was not be the problem the patient told me, but the real problem of what was causing the pain. For instance, a woman came to me for healing with chest pain, she had done the usual trip to the doctor and had the tests but they could not find anything wrong so she came to healing. As soon as she sat down, I saw twin babies sitting on her lap. I put my hands on her shoulders and asked spirit who they were. They told me she had lost the twins through the stress. Her parents wanted the child adopted, but she wanted to keep them.

I carried on with the healing and when I was finished I

asked spirit if it was okay to give her the message as it was clairvoyance and usually healers don't give out messages, but the answer I got back was precise, 'it is not clairvoyance, it is healing and yes, give her the message'.

Therefore, I asked her permission and gave her the message. She was delighted. I told her of the twins sitting on her lap and she burst into tears. She had told no one of that time in her life because she had been too ashamed to do so. Her mother had wanted adoption, as she was a single girl at the time and too young to have any say in the matter, but she desperately wanted to keep them and became ill with the stress of giving them up. In the process she lost the twins and always felt that is was her fault that they died. She often grieved for them and never forgave herself. When she heard they were always with her and loved her dearly, her face lit up and I knew in that instant, her chest pain was going to be just fine. She was going to see her babies again and that in itself was healing.

Some people say you should not give messages after healing, but I say, sometimes the messages are desperately needed and Spirit say these are part of the healing process, so why not, as long as you have patient's permission to do so. To know that a child is just fine in spirit, waiting for you to join it or your mum and dad are still with you can be a great healing experience. Now I know there are some charlatans are out there in the psychic/spiritual world, but a good medium will tell you something they could not possibly find out, a secret you have told no one or a worry you have not shared.

A good medium will not charge you a fortune to tell you a message, but you will want to give them a fortune when you hear the evidence. Try to find out for yourself who is a good medium and who is not. Don't believe the critics who have picked a Rosie Lee kind of medium with tarot cards and a crystal ball and held her up to the world to represent all mediums and healers. Try to discern for yourself what you expect from a healer or medium and if you receive that, then be happy that you have met the one that is right for you.

Another cause of disagreement is whether a healer should charge or not. They have to pay the bills like any other therapist. If they should not charge patients then the same should apply to all therapists. Healing requires training and practice just like any other therapy; it is a person's profession and time so why shouldn't they be paid?

If the argument is that you cannot prove it works or that you cannot feel it work then that is pure nonsense, I have gone to a doctor who could not find a cure but he was still paid for his time. I have had a cream to help a cut heal, but it took time, it was not an instant cure, and he still was paid. Some cures might not even work in the way a patient might expect, but that does not make them useless. For instance, say a doctor gives me pills to cure acne, but the side effect is that they make me put on weight. Should I pay him? The cure was not completely how I thought it would be. Of course, you should. The acne was cured. The weight is just an aftermath of the healing, which can also be rectified.

It is a complicated area, but it should not be. Healing works, but it heals the whole, not the just the wound you can see. It might take time, as the emotional problem might be greater than the wound, but in time, it will heal the bit you *can* see.

When you get an aspirin from the doctor for the thinning of your blood to help prevent blood clots, you do not see the blood being thinned out and may not feel the benefits, but you do trust that it will work. Is this faith in the doctor, the medicine or is it just because we are told it works from the pharmaceutical companies and they can prove it with tests. Of course this is true, they took years of tests and tried it on millions of patients and bingo, they now know it works.

Nevertheless, it took time and a great leap of faith for the patients who first tried it.

Healing takes time, patience and some understanding of the process. One session of healing might not instantly cure ten years of pain instantly, it needs time to unravel all the areas of pain and how best to heal them as a whole. This is true of traditional medicine and alternative medicine also. If I go to a doctor because I have been beaten up, first he cures the cuts and bruises with creams and then the pain with painkillers, but that is only on the surface. The emotional trauma needs healing too but this will need a counselor. You see what I mean, to heal the whole person you will need more than one session to the doctor and therefore more than one session in healing.

Take for instance one girl who came to me for healing. She walked in the door a little bundle of nerves, her hair was completely covering her face, her appearance unkempt ragged. I said hello and she mumbled something inaudible back. She kept her head down and her hair covering her face, so I did not press her for details and began healing.

Whilst healing I saw that her heart chakra was full of tears, like an ocean of pain flowing into every other part of her body. I asked what this was about and my guides told me that she was missing the love and guidance of her mother. They showed me one white rose and one red one. I asked how to help and they just told me to give her hope and a promise that within 24 hours there would be a significant difference.

I had no clue what they were talking about, but at the end of the session, I sat down beside her and asked if I could lift her hair from her face. She nodded and it was instantly obvious why she was so distressed. It was the worst case of acne I had ever seen. Her face was bloody from the gaping pustules that had covered most of her sweet face.

I asked her permission to give her the message I got about

her missing her mother and the two roses. She cried. The two roses were from her sister and herself, one white and one red. Sometimes you find yourself saying things that you just know is Spirit talking through you. I began to tell her about the promise they made, and that it would feel as if the layers of her skin were burning for a few hours, but to bear with it, as this was healing the skin. That she would curse me because she would feel it intensely but to try to let it happen and go to sleep. They said not to put cream on it just some water to cool it, but no cream. They promised that she would go to the mirror the next day and be amazed.

Then her mother came through and told her how proud she was and how she should carry on with college and have faith in what she could do. She told her to stand up straight, wear the pretty clothes she used to wear and try her best to be as happy as she could be. When I was finished with the whole message she was smiling, her hair pushed from her face and she walked out the door with a determination to face the world again. I was thrilled to bits, but also curious as to how the healing was going to work, even though I was assured by spirit that all would be well.

The next day I was hoping that she would come charging through the door, acne completely healed, yelling, 'Wahoo!' but it never happened and I was thoroughly disappointed. Then a week later I was stopped by a girl who smiled and said hello with such friendliness that I was ashamed to have forgotten whom she was. I could not place her and she smiled at me and said, 'You don't recognize me do you?' I did not, but gradually it dawned on me and her eyes lit up. I was flabbergasted. She looked stunning! Her face, completely transformed, her clothes were beautiful, not dark, and unobtrusive, and her hair was back from her face and shining. I was delighted.

She apologized for wanting to beat me up on that first

night, as the burning began, but in the morning, she said she cried buckets of tears when she saw the result. It was pink, beautifully pink and the spots were not bleeding. They were fading fast. "I could see my face for the first time in a long time and not just the acne" she beamed.

I had told her to go to the doctor and ask for some counseling to help her with the loss of her mother and she had done that too. She also enrolled in college and was excited about starting. She wanted to do all these things before she came back to see me and to give the acne more time to heal. She was over the moon and so was I. I am delighted to say I never saw her in the healing room again, so I am sure she made it through that very stressful time in good shape.

Healing usually takes time, but in this case, Spirit knew that the clearing of the acne was a vital step in the healing process and that she would not seek help or go to college if this step was not addressed first. They also knew that if they took this away she herself would seek the healing of her heart and go on to take her place in the world. Therefore, you see, healing will sometimes heal the physical first to bring about a deeper healing later on. It is always the priority of Spirit to heal the person within, no matter what that takes to achieve.

Look at all the elements that went into the healing process: a gentle approach by the healer, a message from mum to give strength and one of hope from Spirit, some guidance of on counseling to help with the grieving process and finally an amazing healing session with spirit when she was at home sleeping.

Therefore, when people say healing does not work, just answer, give it time. I believe healing always works. It works on all levels, and just because you cannot see the instant results, does not mean it has not worked. If you give it time, continue with the healing and seek help from all areas of the medical profession to help you gain healing in mind, body and spirit then you are on the path to healing the whole you and not just the immediate physical.

Personal responsibility comes into play in healing. Say you smoke and you go to the healer to heal your lungs because you cannot breathe. First the healer advises medical assistance and explains that smoke is a toxic influence on the body (it is not his job to tell you to stop smoking as this interferes with free will), and then begins the healing process. Healing is not a quick fix for all the toxins you put in your body, it can help eliminate them, but if you keep putting them back into your body, it is only a matter of time before they take their toll. On the other hand, if you gave up smoking and want to heal the damage, healing can help to do this. You must take responsibility in how you treat your body. You have free will and Spirit will not take that away by healing a person who does not really want to be healed as such. If he really wanted to breathe, he would not put toxic smoke into his lungs. It is a no-brainer really.

Now I know all you smokers out there will say that you started as a child and did not know the dangers of smoking. Spirit understand this, and they also understand addiction and can help you find the courage and strength to get you through this, but if you are not willing to put the work in to heal yourself, then you leave yourself open to sickness and disease. Spirit has compassion, but your body can only take so much and spiritual healing is not the answer to patching up the damage you inflict upon yourself knowingly. That is like a doctor putting plaster of Paris on your broken legs to help them heal, but you keep pulling it off. Your legs will heal in time, but the damage might be so severe as to stop you from ever walking normally again.

Chapter 8

Heal without Healing

Okay, this title sounds odd, how can you heal without healing. I will tell you how. You walk into a large retail store and go the checkout. The girl is anxious, she has been listening to abuse from impatient shoppers all day long, her feet are tired, and her pay does not cover the amount of money she needs to fulfill even one of her dreams. She sits and smiles, takes the abuse and carries on until she goes home.

When she gets home she cries alone at night and no one knows because the next day, there she is again, smiling and being as quick and efficient as she can be. That is not enough for some customers. They are angry because the butter has gone up in price or their partner can't help them bring home the shopping, so they take out their anger on her and go home not even knowing what they have done. To them, she is a servant for their needs, a number, nothing more.

How can you heal this person without actually putting your hands on her shoulders? First, smile at her and if she has a nametag, look at it, see that she is a person and not a number. Help her with your shopping and turn the labels around to help her find the barcode. Make a joke with her and sympathize with her about standing all day long. Pack your own groceries to give her a rest. When you are leaving, say goodbye and wish her a pleasant evening. Say, thank you with a big smile and leave her feeling that you appreciate all the hard work she does all day.

This is healing in another sense. It is your spirit reaching out to hers to tell her that you appreciate her helping you and providing a service. If we all did, she would go home feeling a lot better and not depressed at just another day of abuse from the customers. This goes for all workers who provide us with a service. Give a little, be nice, be gentle, lend a helping hand if you can, do not take your anger out on them because you feel superior or because your boss took it out on you. What goes round, comes round, remember that. Be nice and one day it will come back to you, but even if it does not, be nice anyway. It can help heal the world.

No job is inferior to yours. If you are a brain surgeon, you might not be able to fix a plug, but the electrician can and so you need him and he needs you. Don't think just because you are a brain surgeon that you are more intelligent than him, you may not be, you just know about surgery, he might be an expert in everything but surgery, in fact, he might even be an expert in surgery too but chose a different career because he just doesn't like the sight of blood. The fact is, you never know. As the saying goes, don't judge the book by its cover. Dig a little deeper and know the person that ticks under that nametag we have given him. I once knew a carpenter that was a brilliant artist and a street cleaner that had a degree but loved the freedom of being his own boss and being able to smoke on the job.

If you are going to judge someone, evaluate people on their personality. If you meet a queen and she is a real nasty piece of work will you bow your knee and smile regardless. Yes, of course you will because society has dictated that she deserves this kind of respect. Why, she is not a nice person, why would you be nice to her? On the other hand, society tells you that you do not have to smile at the house cleaner, or even be civil to her, even though she might have the sweetest and gentlest of natures. So you see, treat them according to their nature and not their status in society. Think of this way, would you like the queen to look after your children or the house cleaner?

I know whom I would choose.

I am not saying treat the queen with disrespect and bow and scrape to the house cleaner, not at all, I am saying treat those around you with respect regardless of their job or their status in society. Treat them, as you would want to be treated and be happy in the knowledge that you are doing your bit to make the world a better and kinder place to live.

Another thing that people do is jump to conclusions. Try not to do this, it is silly and makes you look like a fool more often than not. I once knew a professor, who dressed in complete rags, because he did not worry about such things, he was far too interested in learning as much as he could about the world. Do we condemn him for not fitting into our need for society to worry about how they look, or applaud him for *not* being caught up in the rat race of fashion and what society say we should wear to be accepted? I would applaud him.

We see a boy with a hood on and we instantly call him a thug, a hoodie, a gangster, or gang member. We envisage a world of crime and put him down in our judgmental books as a criminal. I know many boys who wear hoods and they are the nicest lads you could meet. They have seen the scowls as they walk onto the bus but it is only their taste in fashion, so please, find out about the boy before you condemn him.

Do you wear a leather jacket, oh no, you must be a Hell's Angel! How about if you wear a short skirt, oh no, you must be a loose woman! What about trainers, oh no, you are a scruff! One famous retail store did not allow you in their shop if you wore them and now you will see the older generation wearing them all the time because they are good for foot support and comfortable to wear. You see what I mean, every generation puts down the next generation through silly, little judgments about their fashion sense and usually it's completely and utterly wrong. Clothes do not say a thing about our personalities they are just clothes.

Hurl out negative energy toward people and they will respond back with negative energy. Smile and you change the energy immediately. Be kind, gentle, and the world becomes a better place around you and therefore spreads to all those around you. Be the beacon of light by showing people that you don't care how they dress, or what their job is or how they do their hair, you just treat everyone with the respect because you know it is the right thing to do. You will find respect when you begin to respect yourself through becoming the best person you can be and not through treating people in a mean, judgmental way. How can you have any respect for yourself as a human being if you mistreat others and hurl abuse at them or judge them as inferior? Be nice and you will like yourself a bit better and therefore like those around you a lot more too. It will become something you crave, to be nice and for others to return this respect and somewhere along this journey love for yourself will grow. When it does, people will begin to notice the new you and treat you with the love and respect you deserve.

If you want to heal the world, this is the way to do it. Heal yourself first, let go of all that negativity from your persona and shine out as a decent human being. Try it, it works because you are changing the energy and the people around you are much nicer and more relaxed and therefore their friends and family are nice and more relaxed and so on and so forth until the circle is complete. What is there to lose, another grumpy day that is all. If you do not like the world you live in, change the *you* that lives in that world, and make a different choice.

There is an old Cherokee saying: A Cherokee chief was teaching his grandson about life, "A fight is going on inside me," he said to the boy. "It is a terrible fight and it is between two wolves. One is evil – he is anger. One is good – - he is joy.

This same fight is going on inside of you." The grandson thought about it and asked, "Which wolf will win?" The old chief replied, "The one you feed."

6th Books investigates the paranormal, supernatural, explainable or unexplainable. Titles cover everything included within parapsychology: how to, lifestyles, beliefs, myths, theories and memoir.